WINNING THE SEO GAME

*PROVEN STRATEGIES FOR GETTING MORE SEARCHES
& TRAFFIC TO YOUR SITE*

DR(HC) RAECHELLE RAE JOHNSON

DISCLAIMER AND/OR LEGAL NOTICES

ACKNOWLEDGEMENTS

Thank you to my biggest cheerleaders; my boys, my son, and nephew-son, for believing I can do anything I want to try. To my two good, good girlfriends, confident, Alisha; Accountability Partner/Assistant (etc), my angel and forever friend, Toni Perkins.

To my family (who doesn't always know what I am doing but are always ready to ride). To each of you for your interest, trust, and continuous support. Thank you for helping to make me a 2nd time best seller and prayerfully a third.

Lastly, but always positioned first and always, and surely having the last word, my Father, Lord and Savior, the Comforter of my soul, "thank you for making a way for this project and many others".

May it be a blessing unto you.

PREFACE

Content creation doesn't have to be difficult; yet sometimes it is. It's the one thing so many businesses struggle with. It's the thing that prevents a large number of businesses from:

- Achieving and maintaining their objective.
- Increasing their revenue and advancing to the next level.
- Amazing launches and selling out all spots.

Here's the deal: A few informative tidbits here and there won't help attract clients or keep your current ones. Promoting whenever or however you want won't provide you the steady 5/6 figure months you want. Without a viable Content Market Strategy, you won't be able to achieve your significant business goals.

What should you do? Show up regularly with high-value material to separate yourself apart from the crowd. STOP creating information that is searchable on Google. Take a fresh approach, give your narrative, and provide new ideas and recommendations to pique people's interest in you, your business, your products, and your services.

In this crowded industry, "*Content Marketing Strategy - Reboot, How to Win Clients and Influence Markets*" will provide you with the tools and knowledge you need to stand out in every manner and design a content marketing plan that establishes you as an expert and converts more dream clients.

Table of Contents

SEO MATTERS MORE THAN EVER

You must understand SEO (Search Engine Optimization) if you want people to visit your website. Here's why:

Social media generated tremendous volumes of traffic 2from 2010 to 2015. You can bet that if you published a blog post with a fascinating title and an eye-catching image, many people would click on it when they saw it on Facebook.

Buzzfeed took advantage of this by producing an unending number of listicles (such as "22 Reasons Seinfeld Is The Best Show Ever"). Many people would come across these items, click on them, and then share them with their social networks.

However, things have altered considerably since then. Facebook (and other social media sites) recognized they were essentially giving businesses free publicity. Shouldn't companies pay to get people's attention?

As a result, Facebook started making it far more difficult for businesses to get people's attention. Previously, a business's post may have been seen by 10,000 people, but now only 1,000 people saw it (not precise numbers, but you get the point). A corporation that wanted a lot of publicity would have to pay for it.

As a result of all of this, gaining as much traffic through social media is becoming increasingly challenging. You must have a large fan base or be willing to pay money.

That is why SEO is so crucial. SEO is the practice of optimizing your website (pages, blog posts, and other content) for search engines like Google. You may acquire a lot of traffic from search engines if you understand it and perform it correctly.

In other words, when people search for specific terms on Google, your site will show near the top of the results. People will come to your website and read your excellent material.

Isn't it straightforward?

In a way. SEO is a simple idea in theory, but it is a little trickier in practice. Of course, this makes sense. There are trillions of online pages out there, and Google must understand them in order to give relevant ones to searchers.

One of the key purposes of SEO is to distinguish your website from the competition. You want your website to be as inviting to Google as possible. The more enticing it is, the more searchers will see it and the more traffic you will obtain.

So, how do you make your website stand out in the eyes of Google? That is the focus of this eBook.

You'll learn real, tried-and-true SEO tactics for improving your Google rankings.

Ready?

Let's begin.

"The Best Place To Hide a Dead Body is
Page Two of Google" - unkn

How Does Google Function?

To comprehend SEO, you must first comprehend how Google functions. The search engine is highly sophisticated, and Google is typically secretive about how it works, but over the years, they've given a considerable bit of critical information.

Google's fundamental purpose is to give relevant information to searchers. Isn't that why we all use it? We are certain that the majority of the time it will yield information relevant to our searches. Nobody would utilize it if it didn't do this consistently. If you search for "dog food" and Google returns results with photographs of fish tanks, you've wasted your time.

To keep users happy, Google is continuously attempting to locate the best, most relevant information for a given search. But how does it determine which online sites are the most useful and relevant?

Ranking Elements

The Google algorithm evaluates approximately 200 different parameters when analyzing pages. These characteristics help Google decide which pages to return in search results. Google examines millions of pages based on their ranking variables when you input a search query to discover the results that best match your search.

Sites with greater "scores" appear higher in search results than pages with lower "scores." The higher a page ranks in search results, the better it is according to all of the different ranking parameters.

Not all ranking variables are created equal, as one might anticipate. Some are far more important than others. So, which are the most crucial? Google has not stated which are the most significant, however there appears to be some agreement on a few:

- Intention to Search
- Backlinks
- It's time to load a page.
- The user encounters
- Content's freshness, richness, and precision
- The site's authority
- Security
- Mobile compatibility
- The data that has been organized
- Optimized voice search

We'll go into much more detail about each of these elements as we proceed through this eBook. Brian Dean's piece Google's 200 Ranking Variables discusses all of the key ranking factors in great depth.

Pay attention to the variables given above if you want to

be successful with SEO. We'll go over each of the factors and what they mean for your website in the pages that follow.

You will have a far better grasp of how SEO works by the conclusion, as well as precise action steps you can do to boost the amount of search traffic your website receives.

SEARCH THE INTENT

Google ranks websites based on search intent. Every search is motivated by a specific goal. In other words, when you type something into Google, you're seeking for a certain result. You're looking for a specific recipe, the height of the Eiffel Tower, or the most current soccer results.

Google will always strive to deliver results that are as close to what you're looking for as possible. Pages that are highly relevant to the search intent will rank significantly higher than those that are not.

You must optimize your pages for search intent if you want to attract search traffic to your website. In other words, you want them to contain the information that people are seeking for.

Assume you own a home improvement website that includes a step-by-step guide to installing a light switch. If you want that page to appear in searches, the information on it should be relevant to the search terms.

So, how should your sites be optimized for search intent?

<u>Keyword Investigation</u>

The act of discovering relevant keywords and phrases with a high monthly search volume and then implementing those words and phrases throughout a page is known as keyword research. Google understands your content better when you include relevant keywords in it.

There are a number of tools available to assist you in locating relevant, high-volume keywords and phrases:

- Ubersuggest
- Ahrefs
- SEMRush
- Long Tail Pro

We'll choose Ubersuggest because it offers many free features, but the other apps are also effective.

There are a few simple strategies for determining the optimal keywords for your page.

To begin, you can immediately insert terms and phrases to determine monthly search volume. Entering "digital marketing" into Ubersuggest produces the following results:

You may see the term, the monthly volume, the cost per click (for advertising), the paid advertising competition, and the typical SEO competition. The higher the level of SEO competition, the more difficult it is to rank on the first page of search results. Extremely high search volume keywords are notoriously tough to rank for.

The idea is to select keywords with a high volume of searches yet little competition.

You'll see a list of related keywords alongside your primary keyword. You should include a few of these in your article along with your major keyword.

Looking at what terms your competitors are already ranking for is another technique to uncover relevant keywords.

Seeing which keywords your competitors rank for will help you select which ones to target. Look for keywords with a lot of traffic but little competition.

Content Optimization

Once you've identified a few important keywords and phrases, *naturally sprinkle them across your page*.

It is crucial not to try to squeeze in as many keywords as possible. This approach, known as "keyword stuffing," is frowned upon by Google and will affect your website.

Think about including your primary keyword:

- The title of this page
- Within the first 100 words
- In a subheading
- Natural scattered across the body

Keep in mind that Google is intelligent. You don't have to use too many keywords. Use them sparingly so that your page's content is obvious without crowding it. It is vital that your page be easy to read and comprehend.

Backlinks are a critical SEO component.

WHAT DO YOU CALL AN SEO EXPERT

WHO CAN'T DRIVE?

A BACKLINK BUILDER

SEO FACTOR #2:
BACKLINKS ARE IMPORTANT

Backlinks are another essential search ranking factor. When another website links to yours, you get a backlink. The more backlinks a page has, in general, the more authoritative and trustworthy it is. Pages with greater authority rank higher in search results.

Thinking in terms of votes could be beneficial. When website A links to website B, it means that the owners of website A think the content on website B is fantastic. It's like a vote of confidence. Additional votes of confidence translate into more links from other websites.

When Google detects a page with a lot of backlinks, it tells them that the page and its content are important to a lot of people. Google ranks pages with a high number of backlinks higher because it believes they are more authoritative and trustworthy.

One need is that the backlinks come from relevant websites. A backlink from an exercise website is a relevant link if you run a jogging website. The content on both sites is related.

If you receive a backlink from a site regarding fish tanks, it is not a relevant link and will be of little value to Google. Google may even consider the link spammy, causing your pages' rankings to suffer.

All of this means that if you want your pages to appear in search results, you must build relevant backlinks to them.

So, how do you go about accomplishing this?

Make amazing content.

While developing amazing content on your website is certainly important, it's not the only factor in obtaining backlinks. Backlinks are external links that point to your website from other websites, and they play a significant role in search engine optimization (SEO) and increasing your website's visibility.

Here are some strategies to obtain backlinks:

1. Create high-quality content: Producing valuable and engaging content is essential. When you provide unique and informative content, other website owners and bloggers are more likely to link to it as a reference.

2. Outreach and guest posting: Reach out to relevant websites and offer to write guest posts for them. In exchange for providing valuable content, you can request a backlink to your website within the post or in your author bio.

3. Broken link building: Find websites in your niche that have broken links, and offer to replace those broken links with links to your relevant content. This helps the website owner by fixing broken links, and you gain a valuable backlink.

4. Influencer collaborations: Collaborate with influencers or thought leaders in your industry. They can mention or link to your content, driving traffic and providing backlinks.

5. Social media promotion: Promote your content on social media platforms to increase its visibility. If your content gains attention and shares, it may attract backlinks from other websites.

6. Online directories and listings: Submit your website to relevant online directories and listings. While some directories may not provide high-quality backlinks, they can still contribute to your website's visibility and potential referral traffic.

7. Monitor and leverage brand mentions: Keep an eye on mentions of your brand or website online. If someone mentions your website without including a link, reach out to them and politely request a backlink.

Remember, the quality and relevance of the backlinks you acquire are crucial. Focus on obtaining backlinks from authoritative and trustworthy websites in your industry, as they hold more value in the eyes of search engines.

Make Excellent Content

The first step toward obtaining backlinks is to develop excellent content on your website. Millions of new web pages are added to the internet every day. It is vital to give individuals a compelling reason to link to your pages. Create useful content that people will want to link to.

What distinguishes valuable content?

A fantastic piece of material will always check at least one of the boxes below:

- It dives more deeply into a subject than previous pieces.
- It has power (facts, studies).
- It is easy to ingest (easy to read, well-designed).
- It is up to date.

For example, if you own a fitness website, would you prefer link to a 500-word listicle or a 5,000-word post authored by an exercise expert? Definitely the latter. It will be significantly more useful to your intended audience than a 500-word puff essay.

Look at what is currently ranking in the search results for a given term if you want to gain backlinks. How are you going to get to the top of those pages? What measures can you take to create more engaging content? It will be difficult to obtain backlinks if you do not want to put in the effort to create high-quality content.

Publicize Your Content

Link building is fundamentally about finding strategic ways to promote your content. After all, in order for people to link to your material, they must first see it.

There are numerous effective methods of promotion, such as:

1. Outreach. Look for websites that are similar to yours. Contact the site owners and ask if they would be willing to connect to your work. You must use caution to avoid spamming. When contacting other websites, use this Email Outreach Guide.

2. Post by a guest. Look for relevant sites that accept guest posts. Include one link to your own website in your message. Make sure to carefully follow any directions offered.

3. Participate in podcasts. Look for podcasts that accept guests. You'll almost certainly get a backlink in the show notes.

4. Locate any broken links. Use an SEO tool like Ahrefs to identify broken links on relevant domains. Send an email to the site's owner, offering your own content as a replacement for the broken link. For further information, see this Broken Link Building Guide.

5. Look for resource pages. Many websites compile lengthy lists of links to useful information. Find relevant resource pages and ask if your stuff can be added.

There are various more strategies for developing links, some of which are more effective than others. Ultimately, they all boil down to the same thing: bringing value to the lives of others.

The more value you can provide, whether through amazing content, guest posting, or locating broken links, the more probable it is that others will link back to your site. Backlinks will come if you provide a lot of worth.

SEO FACTOR #3:
PAGE SPEED IS IMPORTANT

Page speed refers to how quickly a page loads in a browser. Fast pages load almost instantly, whereas slow pages take longer to load. Google is becoming more concerned with page speed these days.

Consider it from their point of view. Searchers will be dissatisfied if they are sent to a page that takes a long time to load. People expect to get results quickly, and if a page takes too long, they'll move on to another.

As a result, they prefer faster pages over slower ones in search results. When all other factors are equal, quicker pages rank higher.

Use the free Google tool Test My Site to see how your site

does in the speed area. It will examine your website, tell you how it is performing, and make precise recommendations for speeding it up.

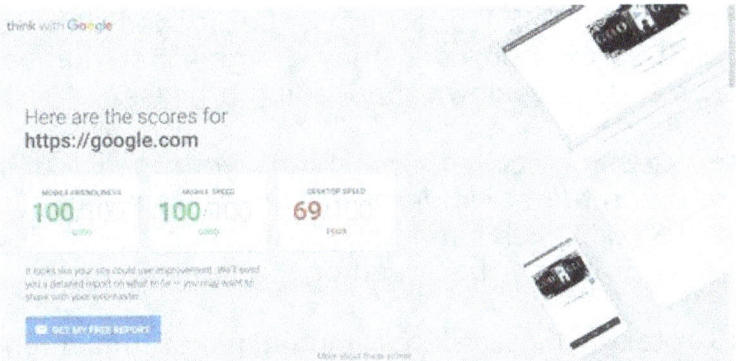

There are a lot of relatively basic things you can do to speed up your web pages in addition to the advice offered by Test My Site. If you are not comfortable doing these things yourself, ask your webmaster if they can assist you.

Image Compression

Large graphics on web pages significantly lengthen the time it takes for them to load. Automatically compressing all of your photographs is a really simple technique to improve page speed. If you're using WordPress, the WP Smush Image plugin will take care of everything.

After you install it, the plugin will scan your media library for images that can be compressed. You can also bulk upload photographs, which WP Smush will compress.

If you don't use WordPress, you may easily compress your images with services like TinyPNG or TinyJPG. Both of

these programs are capable of handling your compression requirements.

Utilize Browser Caching

When someone views your website, all of its parts, such as graphics and HTML code, must be loaded into their browser. This method consumes a significant number of resources and slows down the loading process.

Browser caching caches aspects of your site, such as headers and footers, within users' browsers so they don't have to refresh each time they visit your site. This can significantly improve the speed of your website.

The W3 Total Cache WordPress plugin makes implementing browser caching on your site a breeze.

HTML Should Be Compressed

When someone views your site, their browser must load and comprehend the HTML code. Page speed is increased by reducing the amount of HTML that must be loaded. Minification reduces HTML by cleaning it up: deleting unneeded lines, removing duplicate data, and so forth.

You don't have to be a code genius to minify the HTML on your website. It will be handled by the Minify HTML WordPress plugin. After installing the plugin, go to the settings and enable it. Your page speed will improve as a result of this.

Remove Extraneous Plugins and Scripts

Plugins and scripts are excellent ways to enhance your website's functionality. Regrettably, they might also

degrade its overall performance. The plugins and scripts must be loaded each time your site loads.

Remove any extraneous plugins and scripts to help your page load faster.

Make Use of Content Delivery Network (CDN)

A Content Delivery Network (CDN) distributes your website's files to a vast number of servers around the world (as opposed to servers in a central location). When someone visits your website, the files are downloaded from a server that is relatively close to them.

The physical proximity of the servers accelerates the loading of your websites.

CDNs include the following:
- Cloudflare
- MaxCDN
- Cloudwatch

SEO FACTOR #4:
USER EXPERIENCE (UX)

In recent years, Google has begun to employ RankBrain, a machine learning system, to determine whether people are satisfied with search results. Pages with a high level of user satisfaction appear higher in search results.

RankBrain considers User Experience Signals when determining if a page is fulfilling users. It basically examines how people interact with a page and then ranks it based on those interactions.

If Google sees people interacting positively with your site, your pages will rank higher in search results, and you will receive more search traffic.

How does Google detect if users are having a good time on your site? It considers a variety of factors, including Click-Through Rate (CTR) and Dwell Time.

<u>CTR (Click Through Rate)</u>

The percentage of individuals that view your site in the search results and click over to your site is known as the click through rate (CTR). If 100 individuals visit your site and three of them click through, your CTR is 3%. A high CTR indicates to Google that a page is important and should rank high in search results.

Every Google search result contains three elements: the page title, the page description, and the page URL.

If you want to boost your CTR, you must optimize all three factors for maximum clicks:

1. Begin by improving your page title. It should be eye-catching in order to stand out in search results. People will not click on your page title if it is plain or boring. Your title should make it clear that the page has the content that visitors are looking for and that it is worthwhile to click on.

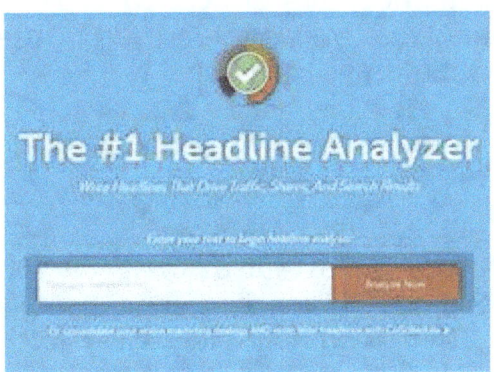

• Use CoSchedule's Headline Analyzer if you're having trouble coming up with good titles. It will review your proposed title and provide suggestions for how to improve it.

2. Then, improve your page description, which is the text that appears beneath the title. It, like your headline, must be both clear and compelling. Include your major keyword in the description so that searchers know the page has the content they're looking for.

3. Third, optimize your page's URL. The simplest approach to accomplish this is to keep the URL short and include the major keyword. For example, www.example.com/primary-keyword. Avoid using long keywords that contain a large number of random characters. Keep them brief and to the point.

Dwelling Time

Dwell time is the amount of time someone spends on your site after clicking on a search result. If people stay for an extended period of time, it indicates to Google that the material on the website is valuable and should be ranked higher in the search results. A longer dwell duration equals a higher rating.

The most effective strategy to enhance dwell time is to develop excellent content that people want to consume. Light, fluffy stuff will not suffice. It's critical to provide visitors with rich information that draws them in from the start and keeps them fascinated until the finish.

There are a few additional things you can do to boost dwell time on your pages:

1. Short, quick introductions. Most intros take way too long to get to the point. When someone sees a website, they want to know immediately away if it

2. can assist them. Keep your introductions short, precise, and to the point. Tell folks what they'll learn first, and then move on to the remainder.

3. Content that is lengthy. Longer, more detailed material performs better than short content. Long content delivers considerably fuller responses than short information, which leads readers to stay on the page longer, which increases overall dwell time.

4. Simple to read. Longform content must be easy to read if it is to be created. Large blocks of text are intimidating and will turn visitors away. To break up the material, use subheadings, paragraph breaks, bullet points, and other techniques.

5. Include videos. Embedded videos can augment the text on your website. Another advantage is that they keep visitors on your pages longer, increasing dwell time.

6. Internal hyperlinks. Linking to additional, highly related pages on your website encourages consumers to explore your site more, increasing overall dwell time.

When you finally get to
the top of Google and
realize it's not as cool as
you thought it would be

BONUS CHAPTER:
THE MORE YOU KNOW

holiday bonuses

Search engine optimization (SEO) is a skill that can help you generate money online. As soon as you mastered the fundamentals, you can begin ranking your own websites for profit.

It takes work learning how to create wealth with this method, but it is a fantastic way to do it. Furthermore, the earning potential for those who use it, SEO constructs high-ranking websites and successfully monetize boundless virtually perpetuated a continuous cycle.

Steps to Create Wealth with SEO:

1. Master the Basics: Learn the fundamentals of SEO, including keyword research, on-page optimization, backlink building, and user experience optimization.

2. Choose a Niche: Select a niche that interests you and has profit potential. Research keywords and competition to identify opportunities.

3. Build High-Quality Content: Create valuable, engaging, and well-optimized content for your chosen niche. This content should provide solutions to users' problems or fulfill their needs.

4. Optimize On-Page Elements: Ensure your website's technical aspects are in order, including meta tags, headers, URLs, and mobile-friendliness.

5. Earn Backlinks: Develop a backlink strategy to acquire high-quality and relevant links from authoritative websites. This helps improve your site's credibility and search rankings.

6. User Experience Matters: Focus on providing a seamless user experience. Fast loading times, easy navigation, and mobile responsiveness are crucial.

7.   Monetize Your Site: Implement monetization strategies such as affiliate marketing, display ads, sponsored content, or selling your products/services.

8.   Analyze and Iterate: Regularly analyze your site's performance using tools like Google Analytics. Adjust your strategies based on data to improve rankings and conversions.

Realistic Earning Potential:

Earning potential through SEO varies widely based on factors like niche, competition, effort, and strategy. Here's a realistic breakdown:

1.   Starting Phase: In the initial months, your earnings might be minimal as you're building your site's authority and traffic. Earnings could range from $0 to a few hundred dollars per month.

2.   Growth Phase: As your site gains traction and ranks higher, earnings could increase to a few hundred to a few thousand dollars per month. This phase might last 6 months to a year.

3.   Established Phase: With consistent effort, quality content, and effective monetization, your site could earn in the range of several thousand to tens of thousands of dollars per month.

4.   Long-Term Potential: For successful websites that dominate their niche and consistently provide value, earnings can surpass six figures annually.

Remember that SEO success takes time, dedication, and ongoing effort. While some achieve substantial earnings, others might see more modest results. Patience and consistent improvement are key to realizing the full earning potential of SEO.

Below are some actionable steps you can take to create wealth with SEO:

1. Keyword Research and Niche Selection:
    a. Conduct thorough keyword research to identify high-volume and relevant keywords in your chosen niche
    b. Select a niche that aligns with your interests, has commercial intent, and manageable competition.

2. Quality Content Creation
    a. Develop high-quality, comprehensive, and engaging content that addresses user needs and questions.
    b. Focus on providing unique value, well-researched information, and solving specific problems.

3. On-Page Optimization:
    a. Optimize your content's on-page elements,

including meta titles, descriptions, headers, and internal linking.

b. Ensure your content is well-structured, readable, and contains appropriate keyword usage.

4. Technical SEO:

a. Ensure your website is mobile-responsive and loads quickly.

b. Create a sitemap and submit it to search engines, and use schema markup to enhance search result visibility.

5. Backlink Building:

a. Develop a backlink strategy to acquire quality links from authoritative websites in your industry.

b. Focus on natural link-building methods, such as guest posting, outreach, and content collaboration.

6. User Experience Optimization:

a. Improve your website's user experience by optimizing navigation, reducing bounce rates, and enhancing site speed.

7. Monetization Strategy:

a. Implement various monetization methods, such as affiliate marketing, selling digital products, offering online courses, or displaying ads.

b. Ensure your monetization methods align with your niche and provide value to your audience.

8. Promotion and Social Sharing:

    a. Promote your content on social media platforms, online forums, and relevant online communities.

    b. Encourage sharing and engagement to increase your content's visibility.

9. Regular Content Updates:

    a. Continuously update and refresh your existing content to keep it relevant and up to date.

    b. Google rewards fresh and valuable content with higher rankings.

10. Analytics and Measurement:

    a. Set up Google Analytics to track your website's performance, user behavior, and traffic sources.

    b. Regularly review your data to identify trends, strengths, and areas for improvement.

11. Continuous Learning:

    a. Stay updated with the latest SEO trends, algorithm changes, and best practices.

    b. Participate in industry webinars, forums, and courses to enhance your skills.

12.Persistence and Patience:

    a. Understand that SEO results take time to materialize. Be patient and persistent in your efforts.

    b. Consistently apply best practices and adapt your strategies based on data-driven insights.

Remember that creating wealth with SEO requires a combination of strategic planning, consistent effort, and adaptability to changes in the digital landscape. By following these actionable steps and staying dedicated, you can increase your chances of building a successful and profitable online presence.

SEO FACTOR #5:
CONTENT FRESHNESS, ACCURACY, AND DEPTH

All content is not created equal, and Google is particularly concerned with providing searchers with relevant stuff. They look at a variety of factors to guarantee they give the finest results.

<u>Freshness Of the Content</u>

If a search is time-sensitive, it must be current and up to date. If someone looks for "current NFL standings," they want the most up-to-date information. They are not interested in NFL standings from six months ago.

If the material on one of your sites changes on a regular basis, it is critical that you do your best to keep it up to date. It will not perform well in searches if you do not.

A longform guide on John F. Kennedy is unlikely to need to be updated on a frequent basis because the information is generally static. Because new laptops are introduced all the time, a list of the best gaming laptops should be updated on a regular basis.

As a general rule, attempt to update your content if the information changes significantly.

Accuracy Of Content

Google makes every effort to ensure that the information displayed in search results is correct. They accomplish this in a variety of ways. They compare information to something known as the "knowledge graph," which is a massive information warehouse containing data on a wide range of topics.

There is additional evidence that Google relies on a variety of reliable online resources to validate information.

The reasons for this insistence on precision are self-evident. You wouldn't want to use Google if it consistently gave erroneous search results. Furthermore, if people act on inaccurate information (such as prescription dosage), the consequences could be disastrous.

Try to double-check the information you publish. If you're unsure about something, consult trusted sources.

Depth Of Content

The more completely you cover a subject, the more likely you are to rank in the top search results. To be clear, thoroughness is not the same as length.

In-depth coverage of a subject means that you supply all of the information that searchers are seeking for.
People will visit your site, not find what they're looking for, and then go to visit another site if you don't properly cover a subject. Your stay time will be short, which Google will interpret as meaning your material isn't relevant, and your rankings will suffer as a result.

Consider all of the many things people might search for in relation to the material you're providing as you develop it. The more topics you cover, the more relevant your material is to searchers.

If you're unsure about what people are looking for, enter your major term into Google, scroll to the bottom, and look at the related queries. This will give you an idea of the topics that are relevant to your primary keyword.

SEO is no longer just a job title it has become part of everyone's job description.

SEO FACTOR #6:
SITE AUTHORITY

Some websites have more clout than others. The Mayo Clinic's website is far more authoritative on medical concerns than any random person's blog. Major news outlets hold more weight than single-person websites.

When it comes to search results, Google favors websites with high authority. These websites, according to Google, are the most reliable sources of information.

What distinguishes an authoritative website? While Google does not have a precise list, there appear to be a few things that everyone agrees on.

Backlinks are the first key to authority. Sites having a large number of backlinks from various sources are thought to have greater authority than sites with a small number of backlinks. We've already discussed backlinks extensively, so we won't go into detail here.

Another factor that contributes to authority is subject matter competence. Google understands that no one person can be an expert in everything. They like sites that focus on being an authority in a specific field.

They state in their SEO Starter Kit:

> A site with a strong reputation is reliable. Develop a reputation for expertise and trustworthiness in a given field...A site's expertise and authoritativeness boosts its quality. Make certain that the information on your website is generated or revised by subject matter experts. For example, providing expert or experienced sources can assist users in understanding the competence of publications. If such consensus exists, displaying it on articles about scientific topics is a good practice.

Focus on building and displaying your knowledge in a specific field if you want your pages to rank in search results. Avoid attempting to cover too many topics. Concentrate on creating the greatest content in your niche.

Instead of focusing on the immensely broad subject of technology, for example, concentrate on one aspect of technology, such as cellphones.

Building a website's authority is all about momentum. The more authoritative material you write, the more backlinks you will receive. More backlinks make your site more authoritative. It gets easier to establish your authority once you get things going.

SEO FACTOR #7:
SECURITY

Security and mobile friendliness are two of the most important SEO factors.

Security and mobile friendliness are two additional ranking elements that you may have already incorporated. It will be extremely difficult for you to rank highly if these elements are not in place on your site.

SECURITY

Google is concerned about its users' security. They don't want to direct people to an unprotected site where their data could be compromised.

If you use the Chrome browser, you may have received a "Not Secure" warning when attempting to access some pages. This warning appears on websites where the data transmitted between the browser and the server is not encrypted.

How can you tell if your website is safe?

A straightforward method is to look in the URL bar where your web address is typed. Depending on your browser, you should see "https" before the web URL or a security indicator (in Chrome, it's a padlock).

If your site isn't secure, use an SSL certificate to make it so.

Let's Encrypt is a free SSL certificate that you may use to secure your website. Your webmaster should be able to assist you if you don't know how to install one of them. Furthermore, many web servers will install one for you automatically.

Mobile Compatibility

In addition to being secure, your site should be mobile friendly, which means it should appear excellent on a smartphone. Mobile-unfriendly websites and pages will perform poorly in search results.

Go to Google Search Console and look at the "Mobile Usability" report to evaluate how your site performs on mobile phones. There, you can check to determine whether your site has any mobile difficulties.

Mobile Usability

Given that mobile phones account for a large portion of online searches, it is critical that your site be optimized for them.

SEO

Removing a comma
from a page that Ranks #1

SEO FACTOR #8:
USE STRUCTURED DATA

Many web sites contain material that is simple for
humans to understand yet difficult for the Google
algorithm to grasp. For example, you may have a product
page that includes information such as prices, availability,
ratings, and more. Unless you organize the material in a
precise way, Google will struggle to grasp it.

Structured data is coding that you add to your pages to
assist Google interpret the information. Structured data
formats exist for a wide range of applications, including:

- Books
- Movies
- Courses

- Ratings
- Events
- Local business information
- Recipes
- And a lot more

Structured data may appear directly in search results if implemented appropriately. Have you ever looked up a piece of content marketing equipment and notice top 3 preferred equip by curators? That is the result of structured data implementation.

Amazon.com: digital cameras
https://www.amazon.com/digital-cameras/s?k=digital+cameras ▾
 Minolta 20 Mega Pixels High Wi-Fi Digital Camera with 35x Optical Zoom, 1080p HD ...
Amazon.com : Minolta 20 Mega Pixels High Wi-Fi Digital Camera with 35x Optical
Zoom 1080p HD Video & 3" LCD Black (MN35Z-BK) : Electronics

A "rich snippet" is information that appears immediately in the results. Rich snippets boost the likelihood of a person clicking on your website in the search results. You can use Google's Structured Data Markup Helper to generate this type of data. You enter the URL of the page you wish to change, and Google will walk you through the process of adding structured data to it. Once finished, just copy, and paste the corrected information back into your website.

SEO FACTOR #9:
OPTIMIZE FOR VOICE SEARCH

Voice search has increased since the introduction of voice assistants such as Siri, Alexa, and Google Home. People can speak their searches instead than typing them in.

It's critical to consider how most people use voice search when optimizing for it. Almost always, it takes the form of a question:

- What is Paul Newman's age?
- When does the movie start?
- Is it safe for dogs to drink cold water?
- When did the Beatles call it quits?

The ideal strategy to optimize for voice search is to offer content that Google can pull and display as an answer to an inquiry.

Some reasonably easy methods are:

1. Make FAQ pages. These pages are typically short and to-the-point responses to a variety of specific questions, which is exactly what Google looks for when providing voice search results.

2. Aim for the highlighted snippet. The featured snippet frequently appears before any other search results and is frequently used as a response to voice queries. Check out HubSpot's post for tips on how to get the highlighted snippet.

3. Write freely. Google prefers content that is written naturally because it wants voice search results to seem natural. In other words, write as though you were speaking. Try not to be stiff and formal.

4. Maintain simplicity. Voice search results are often around a 9th grade reading level. This is one reason why you should avoid using jargon or sophisticated terms.

5. Increase the speed of your website. Google prefers quicker websites in order to offer voice search results quickly. The sooner your site loads, the higher your chances of ranking for voice searches.

Consider the type of information you would want to know and the questions you would ask to get it as you strive to make your site voice-search-friendly. Then, naturally incorporate that information into the material you're generating.

SEO FACTOR #10:
PLAY THE LONG GAME

SEO is a long game that takes time to master. Great content that is optimized for search intent and user experience takes effort to generate. Obtaining backlinks to your website necessitates a persistent, concerted effort.

However, the work is worthwhile. SEO is one of the most efficient methods of driving regular traffic to your website.

We've covered a variety of SEO tactics that you can start using right away:

- Search intent optimization
- Obtain backlinks

- Increase the speed of your website.
- Create a positive user experience
- Create material that is current, accurate, and comprehensive.
- Increase the authority of your website.
- Check that your website is secure and mobile-friendly.
- Make use of organized data.
- Prepare for voice search

SEO isn't all that complicated at its heart. Your goal is to provide individuals with what they are looking for: reliable, authoritative content that is relevant to their search. You want to deliver them this content in the greatest possible format: a website that is safe, mobile friendly, speedy, and easy to consume.

When you focus on offering people what they want in the greatest way possible, acquiring backlinks becomes lot easier.

So, begin playing the long SEO game right now. You probably won't notice results right away, but if you stick with it, you will.

OUR CHECKLIST FOR HOW TO WIN THE SEO GAME

To win the SEO game and improve your website's search engine rankings, there are several key factors and best practices to consider. Here's a checklist to help you:

1. Keyword Research:
   - Identify relevant keywords and phrases that your target audience is searching for.
   - Use tools like Google Keyword Planner, SEMrush, or Moz Keyword Explorer to find popular and low-competition keywords.

2. On-Page Optimization:
   - Optimize your page titles, meta descriptions, headings, and content with target keywords.
   - Ensure your website has a clear and logical site structure.
   - Optimize your URLs to be descriptive and keyword-rich.
   - Include internal links to improve navigation and user experience.

3. High-Quality Content:
   - Create unique, informative, and valuable content that satisfies user intent.
   - Incorporate target keywords naturally throughout your content.
   - Aim for longer-form content (1,000 words or more) when appropriate.
   - Include multimedia elements like images, videos, and infographics.

4. Mobile-Friendly and Fast Website:
   - Ensure your website is responsive and mobile-friendly.
   - Optimize your website's loading speed by compressing images, minifying code, and using caching techniques.
   - Implement Accelerated Mobile Pages (AMP) for faster mobile loading.

5. User Experience and Site Usability:
   - Ensure easy navigation and a clear website structure.
   - Make sure your website is visually appealing and user-friendly.
   - Improve your website's loading speed.
   - Optimize for readability with proper font sizes, colors, and formatting.

6. Technical SEO:
   - Optimize your website's crawlability and indexability for search engines.
   - Use an XML sitemap to help search engines discover and index your web pages.
   - Implement structured data (Schema.org markup) to enhance search engine understanding of your content.
   - Fix broken links, eliminate duplicate content, and improve URL structure.

7. Backlinks and Off-Page Optimization:
   - Build high-quality, relevant backlinks from authoritative websites in your industry.
   - Develop relationships with influencers and engage in guest blogging.
   - Share your content on social media platforms to increase visibility and attract organic backlinks.

8. Local SEO (if applicable):
   - Optimize your website for local searches if you have a physical location.
   - List your business on Google My Business and other relevant online directories.
   - Encourage customer reviews and respond to them promptly.

9. Monitor, Analyze, and Adjust:
   - Track your website's performance using tools like Google Analytics and Search Console.
   - Monitor keyword rankings, organic traffic, bounce rates, and conversion rates.
   - Analyze data to identify areas of improvement and adjust your SEO strategy accordingly.

Remember, SEO is an ongoing process, and it takes time and effort to see results. It's essential to stay updated with the latest SEO trends and algorithm changes to ensure your strategies remain effective.

Just for you!!!
THE MORE YOU KNOW

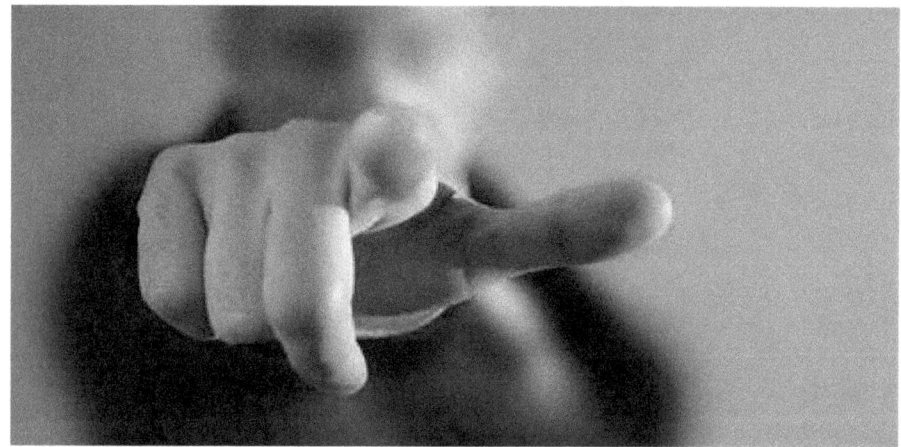

Step-by-step how to implement your checklist for winning the game:

1. Keyword Research:
   a. Use keyword research tools like Google Keyword Planner, SEMrush, or Moz Keyword Explorer.
   b. Identify relevant keywords and phrases that your target audience is searching for.
   c. Consider search volume, competition, and user intent when selecting keywords.

2. On-Page Optimization:
   a. Optimize page titles: Include target keywords and make them compelling.
   b. Craft meta descriptions: Write concise and persuasive descriptions that incorporate keywords.
   c. Optimize headings: Use relevant headings (H1, H2, etc.) with keywords to structure your content.
   d. Optimize content: Create high-quality, informative content that naturally incorporates target keywords.
   e. Ensure a logical site structure: Organize your website into categories and subcategories.

3. High-Quality Content:
   a. Create unique, valuable content: Provide information that satisfies user intent and addresses their needs.
   b. Incorporate keywords naturally: Don't overstuff keywords; aim for a natural flow in your content.
   c. Create longer-form content: Aim for in-depth articles or guides (1,000 words or more) when appropriate.
   d. Use multimedia elements: Include images, videos, infographics, and other engaging media.

4. Mobile-Friendly and Fast Website:
   a. Ensure responsiveness: Design your website to adapt

to different screen sizes and devices.

   b. Optimize loading speed: Compress images, minify code, and enable browser caching.

   c. Implement Accelerated Mobile Pages (AMP): Create mobile-optimized versions of your pages for faster loading.

5. User Experience and Site Usability:

   a. Improve navigation: Ensure easy and intuitive website navigation.

   b. Enhance visual appeal: Use an appealing design, legible fonts, and proper color schemes.

   c. Optimize loading speed: Implement measures to speed up your website's performance.

   d. Focus on readability: Use appropriate font sizes, headings, and formatting for easy reading.

6. Technical SEO:

   a. Optimize crawlability and indexability: Ensure search engines can access and understand your website.

   b. Create an XML sitemap: Help search engines discover and index your web pages effectively.

   c. Implement structured data: Use Schema.org markup to enhance search engine understanding of your content.

   d. Fix technical issues: Address broken links, eliminate duplicate content, and improve URL structure.

7. Backlinks and Off-Page Optimization:

   a. Build high-quality backlinks: Seek relevant and authoritative websites in your industry for link opportunities.

   b. Engage in guest blogging: Write guest posts on reputable websites to gain exposure and backlinks.

   c. Utilize social media: Share your content on social platforms to attract organic backlinks and increase visibility.

8. Local SEO (if applicable):
     a. Optimize for local searches: Include location-specific keywords and information on your website.
     b. List on Google My Business: Create and optimize your Google My Business listing.
     c. Get listed in online directories: Submit your business to relevant online directories for local visibility.
     d. Encourage customer reviews: Monitor and respond to reviews to build trust and improve local rankings.

9. Monitor, Analyze, and Adjust:
     a. Set up Google Analytics and Search Console: Monitor your website's performance and gather data.
     b. Track keyword rankings: Monitor your target keywords' positions in search results.
     c. Analyze traffic and user behavior: Assess metrics like organic traffic, bounce rates, and conversion rates.
     d. Identify areas of improvement: Use data analysis to find opportunities to enhance your SEO strategy

The checklist provided covers the key areas of SEO that are crucial for improving your website's search engine rankings. However, it's important to note that SEO is a complex and ever-evolving field, and there may be additional tactics and strategies that can be employed depending on your specific website and goals.

Some other aspects you may consider in your SEO efforts include:

1. Social Media Optimization:
     - Optimize your social media profiles with relevant keywords and links to your website.
     - Share your content regularly on social media platforms to increase visibility and engagement.
     - Encourage social sharing and engagement with your content.

2. Local SEO (continued):
   - Ensure consistent Name, Address, and Phone Number (NAP) information across all online platforms.
   - Obtain local citations from authoritative directories and websites in your local area.
   - Implement location-specific landing pages or content if you have multiple physical locations.

3. Voice Search Optimization:
   - Consider optimizing your content for voice search queries by using conversational language and long-tail keywords.
   - Focus on answering frequently asked questions related to your industry or niche.
   - Provide concise and direct answers in your content to cater to voice search queries.

4. User Engagement and Signals:
   - Aim to improve user engagement metrics, such as time on site, page views, and low bounce rates.
   - Encourage user interaction through comments, social sharing, and calls to action.
   - Enhance user experience to keep visitors engaged and satisfied.

5. SEO-Friendly URLs and Site Architecture:
   - Ensure your URLs are descriptive, concise, and include relevant keywords.
   - Use a logical site structure with categories, subcategories, and clear navigation menus.
   - Optimize internal linking to establish a hierarchy and guide search engines through your website.

6. Ongoing Content Optimization and Updates:
   - Regularly review and update your existing content to keep it fresh and relevant.

- Optimize underperforming pages by improving keyword targeting, structure, and user experience.
- Conduct periodic content audits to identify gaps or opportunities for improvement.

Remember, SEO is a continuous process, and it's crucial to stay updated with industry trends, algorithm changes, and best practices. Regularly monitoring your website's performance and adapting your strategies accordingly will help you maintain and improve your search engine rankings over time.

When assessing your SEO strategy and performance, here are some important questions to ask yourself:

1. Keyword Strategy:
- Are my target keywords and phrases relevant to my business and aligned with user intent?
- Have I conducted thorough keyword research to identify high-value opportunities?
- Am I incorporating keywords naturally into my content and optimizing on-page elements?

2. On-Page Optimization:
- Are my page titles, meta descriptions, headings, and URLs optimized for search engines and users?
- Is my website structured logically, with clear navigation and user-friendly URLs?
- Have I implemented structured data (Schema.org markup) to enhance search engine understanding of my content?

3. Content Quality:
- Is my content unique, valuable, and relevant to my target audience?
- Am I providing comprehensive and in-depth information that satisfies user intent?

- Are my articles, blog posts, or landing pages optimized for readability and engagement?

4. Website Performance:
   - Is my website mobile-friendly and responsive across different devices and screen sizes?
   - Have I optimized my website's loading speed to provide a fast and seamless user experience?
   - Are there any technical issues, broken links, or duplicate content that need to be addressed?

5. Backlink Profile and Off-Page Optimization:
   - Am I building high-quality backlinks from authoritative websites in my industry?
   - Have I engaged in guest blogging or influencer collaborations to expand my online presence?
   - Is my content being shared on social media and attracting organic backlinks?

6. Local SEO (if applicable):
   - Have I optimized my website for local searches by including location-specific keywords?
   - Is my business listed and optimized on Google My Business and other relevant directories?
   - Am I actively seeking customer reviews and managing my online reputation?

7. User Experience and Engagement:
   - Is my website easy to navigate, visually appealing, and user-friendly?
   - Are visitors spending a significant amount of time on my site and exploring multiple pages?
   - Am I encouraging user engagement through comments, social sharing, or calls to action?

8. Measurement and Analysis:
   - Am I tracking and analyzing key metrics such as

organic traffic, keyword rankings, and conversion rates?
- Have I set up Google Analytics and Search Console to monitor website performance?
- Do I regularly review and analyze data to identify areas of improvement and optimize my SEO strategy?

By asking these questions and evaluating your SEO efforts, you can identify strengths, weaknesses, and areas for improvement. This process will help you refine your strategy and make Data-driven decisions to enhance your website's visibility and organic search performance.

There are several SEO tools available that can assist you in various aspects of your SEO efforts. These tools can provide valuable insights, data, and assistance in optimizing your website and improving your search engine rankings. Here are some popular SEO tools:

1. Google Analytics: A powerful analytics tool that provides detailed data on website traffic, user behavior, conversions, and more. It helps you track the effectiveness of your SEO strategies and measure the performance of your website.

2. Google Search Console: A free tool provided by Google that allows you to monitor your website's presence in search results, submit sitemaps, identify indexing issues, and view search performance data. It provides valuable insights into how Google sees and interacts with your site.

3. SEMrush: A comprehensive SEO suite that offers features such as keyword research, competitor analysis, site audits, backlink analysis, and rank tracking. It provides valuable insights into your website's performance and helps identify opportunities for improvement.

4. Moz: Moz offers a range of SEO tools, including keyword research, site audits, rank tracking, backlink analysis, and on-page optimization. Their tools help you improve your website's visibility, analyze competitor strategies, and track keyword rankings.

5. Ahrefs: Ahrefs is a popular SEO toolset that offers features like keyword research, backlink analysis, content analysis, site audits, and rank tracking. It provides comprehensive data to help you improve your website's performance and visibility.

6. Yoast SEO: A popular WordPress plugin that helps optimize on-page elements, such as meta tags, XML sitemaps, breadcrumbs, and readability. It provides recommendations for improving your content's SEO and readability.

7. Screaming Frog: A website crawler tool that analyzes your site's technical SEO elements, including broken links, redirects, duplicate content, and page titles. It helps identify and fix issues that may impact your website's search visibility.

8. Majestic: Majestic is a backlink analysis tool that provides insights into your website's link profile, competitor backlinks, anchor texts, and link building opportunities. It helps you understand the authority and quality of your backlinks.

9. BuzzSumo: BuzzSumo allows you to analyze content performance and identify popular topics in your industry. It helps you discover trending content, find influencers, and develop content that resonates with your target audience.

10. Google Keyword Planner: A free tool provided by Google Ads that helps you discover keywords, search volumes, and competition levels. It aids in

identifying relevant keywords for your SEO
strategy.

These are just a few examples of the many SEO tools
available. Each tool offers unique features and
functionalities, so it's important to assess your specific
needs and goals before selecting the tools that best fit
your requirements.